The Adventure Begins

_____

_____

My Cruise Trip Daily Agenda

PAGE	DAY	ACTIVITIES	PLACE	DATE

Today's Plans:

_____
_____

Cruise Day #_____
Date: ____ / ____ / ____

Places:

Weather:

Activities List:

_____
_____
_____
_____
_____

My favorite foods & drinks:

_____
_____
_____
_____
_____
_____
_____
_____
_____
_____

My best experience today:

_____
_____
_____
_____
_____
_____
_____
_____
_____

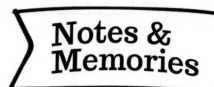

Notes & Memories

Photos & Memorabilia

Photos & Memorabilia

Today's Plans:

_____

_____

Places:

Weather:

Activities List:

_____

_____

_____

_____

_____

_____

My favorite foods & drinks:

My best experience today:

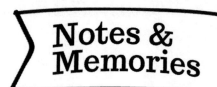

Notes & Memories

Photos & Memorabilia

Photos & Memorabilia

Today's Plans:

_____

_____

Cruise Day #_____
Date: ___ / ___ / ___

Places:

Weather:

Activities List:

_____

_____

_____

_____

_____

_____

My favorite foods & drinks:

_____

_____

_____

_____

_____

_____

_____

_____

_____

_____

My best experience today:

_____

_____

_____

_____

_____

_____

_____

_____

_____

_____

Notes & Memories

Notes & Memories

Photos & Memorabilia

Photos & Memorabilia

Today's Plans:

_____

_____

Cruise Day #_____
Date: ____ / ____ / ____

Places:

Weather:

Activities List:

_____

_____

_____

_____

_____

My favorite foods & drinks:

_____

_____

_____

_____

_____

_____

_____

_____

_____

My best experience today:

_____

_____

_____

_____

_____

_____

_____

_____

_____

Notes & Memories

Photos & Memorabilia

Photos & Memorabilia

Today's Plans:

_____
_____

Cruise Day #_____
Date: ___/___/___

Places:

Weather:

Activities List:

_____
_____
_____
_____
_____
_____

My favorite foods & drinks:

My best experience today:

29

Notes & Memories

Notes & Memories

Photos & Memorabilia

Photos & Memorabilia

Today's Plans:
_____
_____

Cruise Day #_____
Date: ___ / ___ / ___

Places:

Weather:

Activities List:
_____
_____
_____
_____
_____
_____

My favorite foods & drinks:
_____
_____
_____
_____
_____
_____
_____
_____
_____

My best experience today:
_____
_____
_____
_____
_____
_____
_____
_____
_____

Notes & Memories

Notes & Memories

Photos & Memorabilia

Photos & Memorabilia

Today's Plans:

Cruise Day #_____
Date: ___/___/___

Places:

Weather:

Activities List:

My favorite foods & drinks:

My best experience today:

Notes & Memories

Notes & Memories

Photos & Memorabilia

Photos & Memorabilia

Today's Plans:

_____
_____

Cruise Day #_____
Date: ___ / ___ / ___

Places:

Weather:

Activities List:

_____
_____
_____
_____
_____
_____

My favorite foods & drinks:

My best experience today:

47

Notes & Memories

Photos & Memorabilia

Photos & Memorabilia

Today's Plans:

_____

_____

Cruise Day #_____
Date: ___/___/___

Places:

Weather:

Activities List:

_____
_____
_____
_____
_____

My favorite foods & drinks:

_____
_____
_____
_____
_____
_____
_____
_____
_____
_____
_____

My best experience today:

_____
_____
_____
_____
_____
_____
_____
_____
_____
_____
_____

Notes & Memories

Photos & Memorabilia

Photos & Memorabilia

Today's Plans:

_____
_____

Cruise Day #_____
Date: ___/___/___

Places:

Weather:

Activities List:
_____
_____
_____
_____
_____

My favorite foods & drinks:

_____
_____
_____
_____
_____
_____
_____
_____

My best experience today:

_____
_____
_____
_____
_____
_____
_____

Notes &
Memories

Photos & Memorabilia

Photos & Memorabilia

Today's Plans:
_____
_____

Cruise Day #_____
Date: ___/___/___

Places:

Weather:

Activities List:
_____
_____
_____
_____
_____

My favorite foods & drinks:
_____
_____
_____
_____
_____
_____
_____
_____

My best experience today:
_____
_____
_____
_____
_____
_____
_____

Notes & Memories

Photos & Memorabilia

Photos & Memorabilia

Today's Plans:

_____

_____

Cruise Day #_____
Date: ___/___/___

Places:

Weather:

Activities List:

_____

_____

_____

_____

_____

My favorite foods & drinks:

My best experience today:

71

Notes & Memories

Photos & Memorabilia

Photos & Memorabilia

Today's Plans:

_____
_____

Cruise Day #_____
Date: ___/___/___

Places:

Weather:

Activities List:
_____
_____
_____
_____
_____

My favorite foods & drinks:
_____
_____
_____
_____
_____
_____
_____
_____

My best experience today:
_____
_____
_____
_____
_____
_____
_____

Notes & Memories

Notes & Memories

Photos & Memorabilia

Photos & Memorabilia

Today's Plans:

_____

_____

Cruise Day #_____
Date: ___/___/___

Places:

Weather:

Activities List:

_____

_____

_____

_____

_____

_____

My favorite foods & drinks:

_____

_____

_____

_____

_____

_____

_____

My best experience today:

_____

_____

_____

_____

_____

_____

_____

Notes & Memories

Photos & Memorabilia

Photos & Memorabilia

Today's Plans:

_____

_____

Cruise Day #_____
Date: ___/___/___

Places:

Weather:

Activities List:

_____

_____

_____

_____

_____

My favorite foods & drinks:

My best experience today:

Notes & Memories

Photos & Memorabilia

Photos &
Memorabilia

Today's Plans:

_____

_____

Places:

Weather:

Activities List:

_____

_____

_____

_____

_____

My favorite foods & drinks:

My best experience today:

Notes & Memories

Notes & Memories

Photos & Memorabilia

Photos & Memorabilia

Today's Plans:

_____

_____

Places:

Weather:

Activities List:

_____

_____

_____

_____

_____

My favorite foods & drinks:

_____

_____

_____

_____

_____

_____

_____

_____

My best experience today:

_____

_____

_____

_____

_____

_____

_____

Notes & Memories

Notes & Memories

Photos & Memorabilia

Photos & Memorabilia

Today's Plans:

_____
_____
_____

Cruise Day #_____
Date: ___/___/___

Places:

Weather:

Activities List:

_____
_____
_____
_____
_____
_____

My favorite foods & drinks:

_____
_____
_____
_____
_____
_____
_____
_____
_____

My best experience today:

_____
_____
_____
_____
_____
_____
_____
_____

Notes & Memories

Photos & Memorabilia

Photos & Memorabilia

Made in United States
Orlando, FL
27 May 2022